World War II

European Theater

PUZZLE BOOK

USA GRAB A PENCIL PRESS

CARLISLE, MASSACHUSETTS

World War II European Theater Puzzle Book

ISBN: 978-0-9882885-6-0

Published by
GRAB A PENCIL PRESS
an imprint of Applewood Books
Carlisle, Massachusetts 01741
www.grabapencilpress.com

10 9 8 7 6 5 4 3 2 1

Manufactured in the United States of America

World War II
European Theater
PUZZLE BOOK

"We shall defend our island, whatever the cost may be, we shall
fight on the beaches, we shall fight on the landing grounds, we
shall fight in the fields and in the streets, we shall fight in the hills;
we shall never surrender."

Winston Churchill
British Prime Minister

The lead-up to World War II in Europe was driven by German Chancellor Adolf Hitler's
desire for power and additional territory. European powers had turned a blind eye to the
power-hungry German fuhrer, so Hitler had not been stopped from building up his military and taking over other countries, even as Great Britain and France tried to keep the
peace. Once Hitler invaded Poland in 1939, however, a line had been crossed and the
European Allies declared war on Germany. The "Steel Pact," made up of Germany and
Benito Mussolini's Italy, became a commanding force in Europe, invading many countries, including northern France, and committing atrocities against millions of Jewish
people. The Axis powers' fight for domination expanded into the African continent. Hitler
appeared unstoppable.

The turning point came when the United States entered the war and provided a great-
er depth of military and resource support. Unable to overtake Britain by air, beaten down
by Allies in the Battle of the Bulge, outsmarted and forced into retreat in Normandy, and
overrun by the Soviets in Stalingrad, the Germans met final defeat in Berlin. Hitler committed suicide and the Allies claimed victory. British Prime Minister Winston Churchill's
words above proved fateful in that surrender was never an option and defeat of Germany
the final outcome. The war's end brought a shifting of Germany's boundaries and shared
control of the country by the Allies and the Soviet Union.

This book's puzzles feature important battles in Europe, leading figures in the war, the
time line on which major events took place, and a look at intelligence strategies such as
Allied efforts to break the elusive German code.

PUZZLE ANSWERS ON BACK PAGES

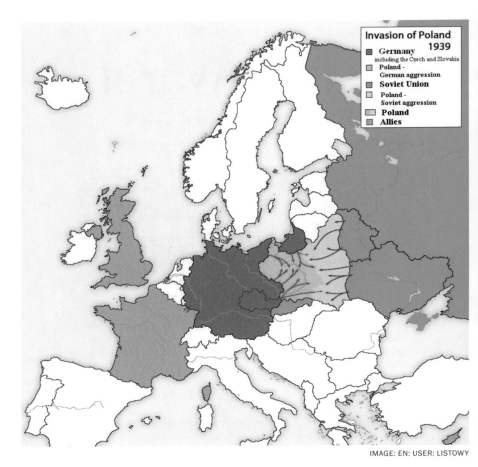

Beginnings of World War II

ACROSS

3. July 10, 1940 — Germany begins air attacks on ___.

4. June 10, 1940 — ___ enters the war as part of the Axis powers.

6. September 1, 1939 — Germany invades ___, beginning World War II.

9. April 27, 1941 — The Mediterranean country of ___ is taken over by the Germans.

10. December 8, 1941 — The ___ ___ enters WWII after the attack on Pearl Harbor.

14. August 25, 1944 — The city of ___ is liberated from German control.

15. June 10, 1940 — The Scandinavian country of ___ falls to Germany.

DOWN

1. June 22, 1941 — Germany and Italy invade ___ with as many as 4 million troops combined.

7. May 15, 1940 — The ___ falls to the Germans.

8. September 3, 1939 — Great Britain and ___ declare war on Germany.

2. September 10, 1939 — ___ joins two European countries in declaring war on Germany.

11. June 6, 1944 — The ___ invasion, called D-Day, takes place on the French coast.

3. December 16, 1944 — The Germans lose a decisive Battle of the Bulge in ___.

12. July 10, 1942 — Allies take the island of ___ in the Mediterranean Sea.

5. September 3, 1943 — Italy falls to the Allies, but Germany helps Mussolini set up a government base in ___ ___.

13. April 30, 1945 — Adolf Hitler commits suicide after Germany loses its final battle in ___.

WARSAW GHETTO UPRISING

Nazi Germany

ACROSS

3. Heinrich ___ was a leading member of the Nazi Party and in charge of the Nazi police.

5. The secret police of Nazi Germany were known as the ___.

7. The ___ resulted in the mass murder of 6 million Jewish people by Adolf Hitler.

8. ___, meaning leader, was the title given to Hitler.

9. Adolf Hitler was elected ___ of Germany in 1933.

12. To provide more "living space" for Germans, the first country Hitler took over was ___ in 1933.

13. The millions who lost their lives were killed by ___ in gas chambers.

DOWN

1. Twenty-three of the most powerful leaders of Nazi Germany were brought to trial for war crimes in ___ following the war.

2. When Germany took over other European cities, Jewish people were forced into fenced-off sections called ___.

4. Leading up to WWII, the Treaty of ___ forced Germany to pay large sums to countries it had fought against in WWI.

6. Jewish people were brought to ___ camps and forced to do hard labor before being killed.

8. German-born youth Anne ___ kept a diary of her life in hiding in Amsterdam, Netherlands.

10. Rudolf ___ was appointed deputy leader of the Nazi Party.

11. As part of the ___ Agreement, Britain and France agreed in 1939 to let Germany have a portion of Czechoslovakia.

US COAST GUARD CREW WATCHES A DEPTH CHARGE EXPLODE IN THE NORTH ATLANTIC

Battle of the Atlantic

ACROSS

3. German ships were tracked by the Allies using ___.

5. Most of the naval action took place in the ___ Atlantic.

10. "U-boat" was short for ___ (undersea boat).

13. The Leigh Light was a ___ used to detect German U-boats that surfaced at nighttime.

14. Germans used U-boats, or ___, to torpedo British ships and sink them.

DOWN

1. Germany had direct access to the Atlantic once ___ had been overtaken in the spring of 1940.

2. Allies attempted to counter the German attack by using ___ for groups of ships.

4. Allies were using the Atlantic to resupply ___.

6. With the prospect of food and military supplies being interrupted, the British prime minister was quoted as saying, "The Battle of the Atlantic was the only thing that ___ me."

7. Prime Minister ___ first used the term "Battle of the Atlantic" in 1941.

8. Allies used ___, new underwater bombs, to destroy German U-boats.

9. German U-boats would attack groups of Allied supply ships in what was called a ___ pack.

11. Breaking German ___ enabled the Allies to track and fight German U-boats.

12. By mid-1943 the United States was able to use the Atlantic to send soldiers and weapons needed for the invasion of ___.

ENIGMA MACHINE

Breaking the German Code

The Enigma Machine looked like a large typewriter and was originally invented by the Germans to send secret messages (ciphers) during the war. Messages were typed on a standard "QWERTY" keyboard; the signal from each letter typed passed through rotors that rearranged the letters. The actual machine was a complex series of wheels with letters that created millions of possible combinations. The British were ultimately successful in understanding how the machine worked and deciphering the German codes. The keyboard below, while not the actual machine, illustrates the complex series of combinations messages had to go through to be decoded.

STANDARD KEYBOARD
Q W E R T Y U I O P
A S D F G H J K L
Z X C V B N M

INPUT

Q W E R T Y U I O P A S D F G H J K L Z X C V B N M
STANDARD

M N B V C X Z L K J H G F D S A P O I U Y T R E W Q
REVERSED

Q W E R T Y U I O P A S D F G H J K L Z X C V B N M
STANDARD

M N B V C X Z L K J H G F D S A P O I U Y T R E W Q
OUTPUT   REVERSED

In the first keyboard line above, a coded letter "P" is typed in (input). In the second (reversed) keyboard line, count over eight spaces to the right from the "P" typed in to get the next letter, "O." From that letter count back five spaces to the left and type "D" in the third (standard) keyboard line. Counting back three spaces to the right on the fourth (reversed) keyboard line will produce the uncoded letter "A" (output). Follow this formula to see if you can decode the missing word(s) in the sentences below.

Electronic _____ were first used in an effort to break German codes during the war.
NSXAFHKJO

The German intelligence agency, _____, produced information that was often ignored by the Nazi Party.   PVLKTJ

The British treated any information they got from the Enigma Machine as _____ top secret.
FWHJP

German spies became British double agents in what was called the _____ _____ Program.
ISFVWK NJSOO

The United States used Austrians and Germans as spies through its intelligence agency, the Office of _____ _____.
OHJPHKYDN OKJBDNKO

The author of the James Bond series of books, _____ _____, worked in British intelligence during World War II.   DPC   UWKXDCY

Sudoku

Solving a sudoku puzzle can be rather tricky, but the rules of the puzzle are quite simple. A sudoku puzzle is a grid of squares or cells. The objective of these sudoku is for each row and column to have all the letters that spell the word at the top of the puzzle. But, you must enter a letter in each cell in such a way that each horizontal row contains each letter only once and each vertical column contains each letter only once.

SHERMAN TANK   PHOTO BY DENNIS JARVIS

TANK

K	T	N	A
A	N	T	K
N	A	K	T
T	K	A	N

NAZI

A	I	N	Z
Z	N	I	A
N	Z	A	I
I	A	Z	N

GERMAN

M	G	E	N	R	A
R	A	N			
E	R	M	G	A	N
A	N	G			
G	E	R	A	N	M
N	M	A	E	G	R

POLAND

O				A	L
		A	D		
L	O				
		D			N
D					
		O			

UNIFORMS

	U	S	I			N	
					I		F
	R			N	S	F	
N	I		S				
O				I		R	
	F	N			U		O
S				M			
		R	F	U		I	

RADIOMEN

N		I					O
E				I			N
	E				O		
	D	O	I		N		M
I		R		O		E	
D					R	N	
		N	M			O	E
O	R		E				A

AIRCRAFT SPOTTER, LONDON

Battle of Britain

ACROSS

5. Hitler's bombing of London stopped when his fighters were needed in attacking ___.

6. After beginning with air attacks on the RAF, Germany focused more on cities, especially ___.

7. Germany's first goal was to stop supplies from reaching Britain by attacking the English ___.

9. The Hawker ___ was the slower but sturdier British aircraft used to defend the homeland.

12. Germany's air force was called the ___.

14. One of the main fighter craft used by the British was the ___ Mk.

DOWN

1. The Stuka and ___ Bf109 were the fighter aircraft used by Germany in the Battle of Britain.

2. The British Royal Air Force was led by Sir Hugh ___.

3. British Prime Minister Winston Churchill said the Battle of ___ was over and the Battle of Britain about to begin.

4. Sergeant Ray Holmes of the Royal Air Force clipped the wing of a German fighter that was heading for Buckingham ___.

5. Despite Germany having more planes and pilots, British ___ tracked when and where attacks were to take place.

8. Operation Sea ___ was Hitler's name for the British invasion.

10. The Germans goal in the Battle of Britain was to destroy the ___ Air Force.

11. Hermann ___ was the leader of the German air force.

13. Some 57 nights of continuous bombing of London was called the ___.

WINSTON CHURCHILL BY WILLIAM TIMYM

TANK AND INFANTRYMEN IN THE SNOW NEAR HERRESBACH, BELGIUM

Battle of the Bulge

ACROSS

4. In the Battle of the Bulge, German spies were dropped behind Allied lines wearing American ___ in an effort to confuse the Allies.

5. Battle of the Bulge took place in the Ardennes forest in ___.

6. The Battle of the Bulge was Germany's last attempt to drive ___ forces from Europe.

8. The battle came as a surprise to Allied forces, as British commander Bernard Montgomery had told General ___ that the Germans weren't capable of mounting a major battle.

10. After the first attack, General ___'s Third Army received backup troops.

12. Germany launched the Battle of the Bulge after defeat at ___, France, and the country being freed.

DOWN

1. Adolf Hitler's ___ advised against going into the Battle of the Bulge.

2. "This is undoubtedly the greatest American battle of the war," proclaimed Winston ___.

3. Due to the snowy weather in which the battle was fought, soldiers wore white to ___ against the Germans.

5. Where German forces pushed back the Allies on a map looked like a ___.

6. Some 2,500 ___ American troops were used by the U.S. military to help fight in the Battle of the Bulge.

7. American bombs attacked fuel ___, causing German tanks to grind to a halt.

9. Hitler's ill-fated mission, called the Battle of the Bulge by Allied forces, was called Operation Watch on the ___ by the Germans.

11. More than 200,000 troops and 1,000 ___ were used by the Germans in driving back unprepared Allied armies.

12. At Bastogne, U.S. General Anthony McAuliffe replied, "___," when ordered by the Germans to surrender or die.

Battle of Normandy (D-Day)

ACROSS

2. Field Marshal Erwin ___ commanded German forces during the Normandy invasion.

4. British Field Marshal Bernard ___ led all Allied ground forces during the Normandy battle.

5. General ___ gave the go-ahead for the attack at Normandy.

8. Allied troops of the U.S., Britain, France, and ___ led the D-Day invasion in France.

9. The June 6, 1944, invasion at ___ Beach met with fierce fighting from Germans and the loss of many lives.

11. More than 160,000 troops crossed the English ___ to fight in the D-Day battle.

12. While Allied bombing was taking place in France, the French ___ cut telephone lines and destroyed rail lines used by Germans.

13. Allied forces' storming of ___ Beach was met with less resistance from German armies.

14. Operation ___ was the name given the invasion of Normandy beaches.

DOWN

1. Troops and equipment were staged in ___ leading up to the Battle of Normandy.

3. The D-Day invasion was called Operation ___.

4. While June 6th is termed D-Day, D-Day is a standard ___ term meaning the day of a major attack.

6. The invasion of Normandy in France was almost canceled due to bad ___.

7. Army Lieutenant General Omar ___ led U.S. ground forces on D-Day.

8. Germans knew an invasion was coming but thought it would be north of Normandy at Pas de ___.

10. The first line of attack on D-Day was paratroopers jumping from planes using ___.

Leaders and Their Titles

1. Dwight D. Eisenhower   ___ a. Fuhrer

2. Erwin Rommel   ___ b. Prime Minister

3. Benito Mussolini   ___ c. German Field Marshal

4. Charles de Gaulle   ___ d. Allied Supreme Commander

5. Bernard Montgomery   ___ e. General /President

6. Adolf Hitler   ___ f. Army General

7. George Patton   ___ g. Marshal/General

8. Joseph Stalin   ___ h. British Field Marshal

9. Winston Churchill   ___ i. General Secretary

10. Georgy Zhukov   ___ j. Il Duce

DWIGHT D. EISENHOWER; GEORGE S. PATTON

OMAHA BEACH, NORMANDY

Names and Places of WWII

```
C L L I H C R U H C H A M A S E
A S I N E R E S T O N H R E T L
N O V I G E R M A N Y N I T A E
S A K A P T L I R S N S B E L M
T N Z T A S H T M A E T A W I M
I H N I T E N S T N G I R A N O
R T E R T A S L H O R B E R G R
S I A B O N R O A C T G L E R N
N W I L N C W P R H I E T I A R
O E R C Y E H S O E A H I T D E
A M A H R T I C A L H M H A R B
I N I L O S S U M R A A O N D E
T R O U N D E R A S T N E L E R
I M S C R I G E N O W E D B R L
R E A T E M O N T G O M E R Y I
B Y D N A M R O N E R Y R O H N
```

Find the following:

NORMANDY	POLAND	MUSSOLINI	ROMMEL
BERLIN	PATTON	ITALY	GERMANY
HITLER	EISENHOWER	OMAHA	BRITAIN
STALINGRAD	MONTGOMERY	NAZI	CHURCHILL

Battle of Berlin

THE REICHSTAG MUSEUM AFTER THE BATTLE OF BERLIN

ACROSS

1. Adolf Hitler's wife, Eva ___, took her life at the end of Berlin's defeat.

4. The Battle of Berlin was fought primarily between German and ___ armies.

5. The Russian flag was raised above the German ___ at the end of the 17-day battle.

7. Some 45,000 Berliners defending the city during the battle were either elderly or ___.

10. The command and defense of Berlin was led by ___.

12. As the opposition entered the city, the German leader committed ___.

DOWN

1. Early in the battle there was ___ of the city by the Russians.

2. Historians feel Stalin hurried to defeat the Germans so that ___ secrets could be kept out of Allied hands.

3. General ___, commander of German troops in Berlin, surrendered the city to the Russian army.

6. The Battle of Berlin resulted in the ___ of the German army on May 7, 1945.

8. Fighting alongside Soviet forces were 150,000 ___.

9. The supreme commander of the Soviet army was Georgy ___.

11. Before entering Berlin, Russian troops attacked Germans at the ___ River.

CROWDS OF FRENCH PATRIOTS LINE THE CHAMPS ELYSEES AFTER LIBERATION, LIBRARY OF CONGRESS

War in Europe Trivia

ACROSS

1. ___ was the type of government run in Germany and Italy.

4. The ___ Front was fighting involving the Soviet Untion.

5. Queen ___ refused to leave England during the German air attacks on London.

6. Navy fighter pilots in Europe used the term "___" to acknowledge and understand direction from the ground.

10. The ___ Machine made by the Germans to send coded messages was successfully decoded by British scientists.

12. German Sophie ___ was considered a war hero for opposing the Nazi Party and the war and was executed for her resistance.

13. Named for the U.S. secretary of state, the ___ Plan supplied Western Europe with $13 billion for recovery from the war.

14. ___ in Europe, or V-E, Day–May 8, 1945, marked the end of the war in Europe.

DOWN

2. ___ remained neutral during WWII and Hitler decided against attacking it due to its being very mountainous.

3. The fighting in the south of Europe was considered the ___ Front.

7. Britain and France's attempt to keep peace with Germany was known as ___.

8. The Soviet Union called fighting on the Eastern Front the Great ___ War.

9. Brigadier General and future president Charles ___ led the government of Free France from Britain.

11. The German army was called the ___.

PUZZLE ANSWERS

Beginnings of World War II

Nazi Germany

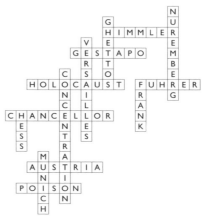

Battle of the Atlantic

Breaking the German Code

computers
Abwehr
ultra
Double Cross
Strategic Services
Ian Fleming

Sudoku

NAZI

A	I	N	Z
Z	N	I	A
N	Z	A	I
I	A	Z	N

TANK

K	T	N	A
A	N	T	K
N	K	A	T
T	A	K	N

GERMAN

M	G	E	N	R	A
R	A	N	M	E	G
E	R	M	G	A	N
A	N	G	R	M	E
N	E	R	A	G	M
G	M	A	E	N	R

POLAND

O	D	P	N	A	L
N	L	A	D	P	O
L	O	N	A	D	P
P	A	D	L	O	N
D	P	L	O	N	A
A	N	O	P	L	D

UNIFORMS

F	U	S	I	R	O	N	M
R	M	O	N	S	I	U	F
U	R	M	O	N	S	F	I
N	I	F	S	O	R	M	U
O	S	U	M	I	F	R	N
I	F	N	R	M	U	S	O
S	N	I	U	F	M	O	R
M	O	R	F	U	N	I	S

RADIOMEN

N	A	I	R	M	E	D	O
E	O	M	D	I	A	R	N
M	E	A	N	D	O	I	R
R	D	O	I	E	N	A	M
I	N	R	A	O	M	E	D
D	M	E	O	A	R	N	I
A	I	N	M	R	D	O	E
O	R	D	E	N	I	M	A

Battle of Britain

```
        M                 D   F
        E             P   O   R
      R U S S I A      W   A
      A   E       L O N D O N
      D   R       A     I   C
      A   S       C H A N N E L
  H U R R I C A N E       G   I
      O   H               O   O
      Y   M         G     N
      A   I         O
      L U F T W A F F E R   B
          T         R       L
            S P I T F I R E I
                    N       T
                    G       Z
```

Battle of the Bulge

```
        G   C                 C
        E   H                 A
        N   U N I F O R M S    M
        E   R                 O
        R   C                 U
        A   H                 F
  B E L G I U M       A L L I E D
  U     S   I         F     A   E
  L         L         R     G   P
  G                   E I S E N H O W E R
  E                   I     T       H
                      C     S       I
            P A T T O N               N
                      A               E
      N O R M A N D Y
      U             K
      T             S
      S
```

Battle of Normandy (D-Day)

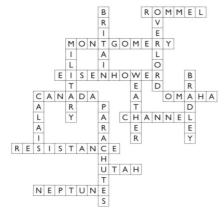

```
          B         R O M M E L
          R         V
          I         E
      M O N T G O M E R Y
      I     A       L
      L     A       O
    E I S E N H O W E R     B
      T     E       D       R
  C A N A D A         O M A H A
  A       R   P       A       D
  L       Y   A   C H A N N E L
  A           R       E       E
  I           A       R       Y
  R E S I S T A N C E
              H
              U T A H
              T
  N E P T U N E S
              E
              S
```

Leaders and Their Titles

1 = d
2 = c
3 = j
4 = e
5 = h
6 = a
7 = f
8 = i
9 = b
10 = g

Names and Places of WWII

```
C L L I H C R U H C H A M A S E
A S I N E R E S T O N H R E T L
N O V I G E R M A N Y N I T A E
S A K A P T L I R S N S B E L M
T N Z T A S H T M A E T A W I M
I H N I T E N S T N G I R A N O
R T E R T A S L H O R B E R G R
S I A B O N R O A C T G L E R N
N W I L N C W P R H I E T I A R
O E R C Y E H S O E A H I T D E
A M A H R T I C A L H M H A R B
I N I L O S S U M R A A O N D E
T R O U N D E R A S T N E L E R
I M S C R I G E N O W E D B R L
R E A T E M O N T G O M E R Y I
B Y D N A M R O N E R Y R O H N
```

Battle of Berlin

```
                    B R A U N
                    O       U
                    M       C
                    B       L
        W     S O V I E T   E
        E         N         A
  R E I C H S T A G         R
        D         U
        L         R
  C H I L D R E N R
        N         E
        G         N
            P     D
  Z         O     E
  H I T L E R     R   O
  U         I         D
  K     S U I C I D E E
  O         H
  V
```

War in Europe Trivia

```
  F A S C I S M
    W         E A S T E R N
    I         D
    T         I
E L I Z A B E T H
    E         E
    R O G E R
    L         R       A       P
    A         R   D   P       A
    N         A   E   P   E   T
    D         E N I G M A     R
        W     A   A   U   S C H O L L
        E     N   U   L         T
  M A R S H A L L   E           I   C
        H             E
  V I C T O R Y
        T
```

TITLES FROM
GRAB A PENCIL PRESS

Abraham Lincoln Crossword Puzzles
American Flag Puzzle Book
American Revolution Crossword Puzzles
Architecture Crossword Puzzles
Art History Puzzle Book
Benjamin Franklin Puzzle Book
Civil War History Crossword Puzzles
Ellis Island and the Statue of Liberty Crossword Puzzles
First Ladies Crossword Puzzles
George Washington Crossword Puzzles
John Fitzgerald Kennedy Crossword Puzzles
Library of Congress Puzzle Book
Natural History Activity Book
New York City Crossword Puzzles
Presidents of the United States Crossword Puzzles
Texas History Crossword Puzzles
Washington, D.C., Puzzle Book
World War II Puzzle Book
World War II European Theater Puzzle Book
Yellowstone National Puzzle Book

COMING SOON
National Parks Puzzle Book
Secret Writing: A Codebreaker's Puzzle Book
World War II Pacific Theater Puzzle Book

USA GRAB A PENCIL PRESS

an imprint of Applewood Books
Carlisle, Massachusetts 01741
www.grabapencilpress.com

To order, call: 800-277-5312